I Like Biographies!

Read About
Abraham
Lincoln

Stephen Feinstein

Enslow Publishers, Inc.

40 Industrial Road	PO Box 38
Box 398	Aldershot
Berkeley Heights, NJ 07922	Hants GU12 6BP
USA	UK

http://www.enslow.com

Words to Know

Civil War—The war between the Northern and Southern states of the United States from 1861 to 1865.

log cabin—A small house made of logs.

slave—A person who works for someone else against their will. Slaves have no freedom.

lawyer—Someone who knows all about the law and goes to court to argue cases before a judge.

Library of Congress Cataloging-in-Publication Data

Feinstein, Stephen.
　　Read about Abraham Lincoln / Stephen Feinstein.
　　p. cm. — (I like biographies!)
　　Includes bibliographical references and index.
　　ISBN 0-7660-2298-6
　　1. Lincoln, Abraham, 1809–1865—Juvenile literature.
2. Presidents—United States—Biography—Juvenile literature. I. Title. II. Series.
　　E457.905.F45 2004
　　973.7'092—dc22
　　　　[B]
　　　　　　　　　　　　2004000508

Printed in the United States of America

10 9 8 7 6 5 4 3 2 1

To Our Readers: We have done our best to make sure all Internet Addresses in this book were active and appropriate when we went to press. However, the author and the publisher have no control over and assume no liability for the material available on those Internet sites or on links to other Web sites. Any comments or suggestions can be sent by e-mail to comments@enslow.com or to the address on the back cover.

Illustration Credits: All photos are from the Library of Congress, except for the following: Corel Corp., p. 21; Enslow Publishers, Inc., p. 19; Painet, Inc., p. 5.

Cover Illustration: Library of Congress

Contents

1 Growing Up in a Log Cabin 4

2 Hard Work for Abraham 8

3 Becoming a Lawyer 14

4 President Abraham Lincoln 18

Timeline 22

Learn More 23

Index 24

Abraham Lincoln was born on February 12, 1809, in Kentucky. His family lived in a log cabin. When Abraham was six, he and his sister Sarah went to school. They had to walk two miles each way.

This is the log cabin that Abraham Lincoln was born in.

The school had only one room. Children from every grade were taught in the same room. Abraham learned to read and write a few words.

The next year the family moved to a new farm in Indiana. There, Abraham helped his father build a log cabin. The nearest town was many miles away.

In Indiana, the school was too far away, so Abraham taught himself to read.

Chapter 2

Hard Work for Abraham

Abraham was good with an axe. He worked for farmers, cutting down trees and splitting logs. Abraham always carried a book with him, even when he worked in the fields. He read all kinds of books. He liked law books best of all.

Abraham was strong. He worked hard cutting down trees and splitting them into logs.

When he was nineteen, Abraham worked on a riverboat. He traveled to many cities. In New Orleans, he watched white people buy and sell black people at the slave market. Abraham thought that was wrong.

When Abraham saw black people being sold as slaves, he thought it was wrong.

When Abraham was twenty-one, he worked in a store in Illinois. He was so honest that people called him Honest Abe. When people had problems, they asked him for advice. So Abraham decided to become a lawyer. He wanted to use the law to help people.

Abraham did not have a beard when he was a young man. He grew a beard after a little girl wrote to him. She told him he would look better with one.

13

Chapter 3

Becoming a Lawyer

In 1834, Abraham Lincoln got elected to the Illinois General Assembly. He kept on studying law. In three years, he opened his own law office. He was elected to the U.S. House of Representatives in 1846.

In 1842, Abraham married Mary Todd. They had four children. They are shown here with their sons Tad, Robert, and Willie.

In 1858, Lincoln ran for the U.S. Senate against Stephen A. Douglas. Lincoln and Douglas argued about slavery. Lincoln was against slavery. Douglas was in favor of it. Lincoln lost that election. But in 1860, Lincoln ran against Douglas and was elected president of the United States.

Abraham Lincoln was the sixteenth president of the United States.

People in the South were afraid that President Lincoln would free the slaves. So the southern states left the Union. Lincoln led the North in a war to keep the South. The Civil War made Lincoln sad, but slavery also made him sad. In 1862, Lincoln wrote an important paper that freed the slaves.

This map shows the Northern states (the Union) and the Southern states (the Confederacy). These two sides fought the Civil War.

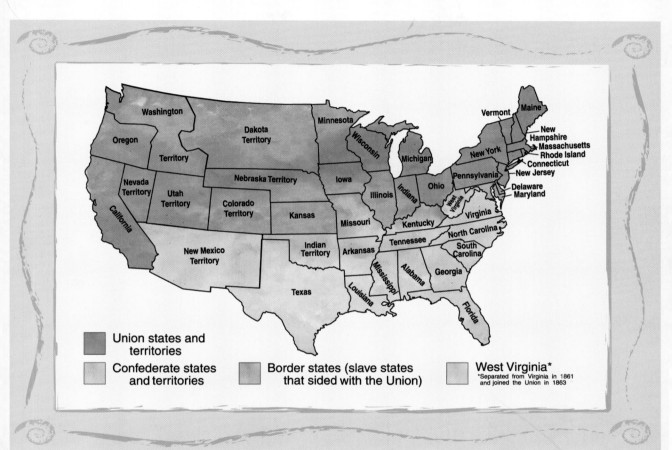

Washington
Oregon
Territory
Dakota
Territory
Minnesota
Wisconsin
Michigan
Vermont
Maine
New
Hampshire
Massachusetts
Rhode Island
Connecticut
New Jersey
New York
Nevada
Territory
Utah
Territory
Nebraska Territory
Iowa
Illinois
Indiana
Ohio
Pennsylvania
Delaware
Maryland
California
Colorado
Territory
Kansas
Missouri
Kentucky
West
Virginia
Virginia
New Mexico
Territory
Indian
Territory
Arkansas
Tennessee
North Carolina
South
Carolina
Texas
Louisiana
Mississippi
Alabama
Georgia
Florida

Union states and
territories

Confederate states
and territories

Border states (slave states
that sided with the Union)

West Virginia*
*Separated from Virginia in 1861
and joined the Union in 1863

19

The war ended on April 9, 1865. The Union was saved.

Five days later, President Lincoln and his wife went to see a play. As they watched, a man shot Lincoln in the head. The president died the next morning. A train carried the body of Abraham Lincoln, one of America's greatest presidents, back to Illinois.

This statue of Lincoln is at the Lincoln Memorial in Washington, D.C. Abraham Lincoln is remembered as one of our greatest presidents.

Timeline

1809—Abraham Lincoln is born in Kentucky on February 12.

1830—Abraham moves to Illinois.

1834—Abraham is elected to the Illinois General Assembly.

1842—Abraham marries Mary Todd.

1846—Abraham is elected to the U.S. House of Representatives.

1858—Abraham runs against Stephen A. Douglas for the U.S. Senate but loses.

1860—Lincoln is elected president of the United States.

1861—The Civil War begins.

1863—Lincoln frees the slaves.

1865—The Civil War ends.

1865—President Lincoln is shot on April 14; he dies the next day.

Learn More

Books

Fritz, Jean. *Just a Few Words, Mr. Lincoln: The Story of the Gettysburg Address*. New York: Grosset & Dunlap, 1993.

Mara, Wil. *Abraham Lincoln*. New York: Children's Press, 2002.

Walker, Pamela. *Abraham Lincoln*. New York: Children's Press, 2001.

Internet Addresses

The History Place Presents Lincoln
<http://www.historyplace.com/lincoln/>

Abraham Lincoln for Primary Children
<http://www.siec.k12.in.us/~west/proj/lincoln/>

Abraham Lincoln Presidential Library & Museum
<http://www.alincoln-library.com>

Index

Civil War, 18, 20

Douglas, Stephen A., 16

Illinois, 12, 14
Indiana, 6

Kentucky, 4

Lincoln, Abraham
    as a lawyer, 12, 14
    as a storekeeper, 12
    childhood, 4, 6, 8
    political career, 14,
        16, 18, 20

Lincoln, Mary Todd, 14,
    20
Lincoln, Robert, 14
Lincoln, Sarah, 4
Lincoln, Tad, 14
Lincoln, Willie, 14
log cabin, 4, 6

New Orleans, 10

slavery, 10, 16, 18